Steps
to a
Happier
Life

by

John Richard Marsh

Copyright

Copyright © 2020 by John Richard Marsh (O'Brien)

All rights reserved. No part of this publication may be reproduced, distributed, or transmitted in any form or by any means, including photocopying, recording, or other electronic or mechanical methods, without the prior written permission of the publisher, except in the case of brief quotations embodied in critical reviews and certain other noncommercial uses permitted by copyright law. For permission requests, write to the publisher, at "Attention: Permissions Coordinator," at the address below.

Although every precaution has been taken to verify the accuracy of the information contained herein, the author and publisher assume no responsibility for any errors or omissions. No liability is assumed for damages that may result from the use of information contained within.

Printed in the United States of America

First Printing, 2020

IngramSpark ISBN: 978-1-7322904-5-7

JRM Productions

John Richard Marsh Productions
1200 Paseo Camarillo, Suite 250
Camarillo, CA 93010
Facebook: john.obrien.3726
www.JRM-Production.com
Cover & Interior Design: Carol Malone
Editor: Judith Mathison,
Creative Consultant/Ghostwriter: Carol Malone

DEDICATION and ACKNOWLEDGMENTS

To my wife: Claudia (Jane) O'Brien, A.K.A. Sunshine. She has inspired me to enjoy life and all I have been blessed with.

To my family who have loved me in spite of the challenges I put them through.

To my friends who accept me for who I am.

Thank you for the opportunity to live a happier life.

I acknowledge with gratitude Rod Brown, without whom I would not have been able to follow my dream of writing and publishing books.

And my thanks to Carol Malone, who takes my story ideas and turns them into manuscripts.

Contents

Good Health 1
Understanding Yourself 4
Becoming The BEST You 6
Achieving Real and Lasting Happiness 8
Financial Security 10
Your Value and Worth 12
The Value of Education 14
The Expense of Living 16
Quality of Life, Morals, and Values in Life 18
Achieving Success in Life 20

Steps to a Happier Life

The following

information reflects

the knowledge and wisdom

I've gained over my lifetime.

I desire to share them with you,

my friends, in the hopes you'll find

something you could identify with or

use to make your life happier, your attitude

positive, and fill your life and hearts with love.

Watch that first step

John Richard Marsh

Good Health
Physical and Mental

1. Good mental health is what keeps everything working in your life.
2. Focus on the positive and explore ways to make the hard changes.
3. Physical and mental well-being requires effort. To keep all your body parts working, your mind functioning, find exercises you like and do them every day. And don't forget to exercise your mind.
4. What you do to your body every day will result in good or bad physical or mental health.
5. Nutritional food fuels the body, keeps it working properly, and helps you to feel your best.
6. Like a paycheck, feeling good is earned one minute, hour, day, month, and year at a time.
7. Smart choices will help you determine what kind of a day you're going to have.
8. Healthy is a place you choose to go, not a place you're sent.
9. The body's strengths are a result of yesterday's positive decisions, so take advantage of the opportunities when they present themselves.
10. If you want better health, it's your decision. Change your mindset and move forward. Nothing and no one can make you happy. Happiness is a choice. Today is the first day of the rest of your life.

No one

is perfect.

No one is ever

Constantly in good

health. You can do better

at working toward your healthy

goals. You can be gentle and kind

to yourself. You can attempt to do your

best each day of your lives, choose wisely

what will keep you at your physical and mental

effectiveness, and take the positive steps you need

to be consistently changing.

Understanding Yourself

11. You are the most important person in your life.
12. Learn to love yourself. Knowing and accepting the real you will serve you well.
13. Remember all the things you are grateful for even during difficult times.
14. Do your best. Having purpose and goals are what you can strive for. Seek help if you need it. Fulfillment is not a place you can arrive at by yourself.
15. Don't sell yourself short. Feeling good is a place you achieve as you move beyond the struggles of our past.
16. If you serve others, you'll worry less about your own troubles.
17. You can be a gift to the world. Share your experiences – good and bad – teach from your heart.
18. You can influence a thousand people in a lifetime, help them love themselves.
19. Help your family and friends achieve their goals in life; be an example of positive change.
20. Plan for and achieve your goals – one day at a time.

Understanding
yourself can bring
positive rewards. Enduring
both good and bad experiences
make your life worthwhile as you pass
through pain and triumph. The person you
become will develop with your efforts to improve,
sacrifice, and a lifetime of work to find your happiness.

Becoming The BEST You

21. What you dream about becoming begins with making good decisions. Your choices to take the steps to improve will get easier with time. You'll eventually become the person you want to be and your life will get better.

22. Becoming what you want to be is a life-long journey. Start today.

23. Change involves imitating the best qualities in other people who have achieved your ideal. Mirror them, don't envy them.

24. People make mistakes. Learn from them and don't make those mistakes yourself.

25. If your life has major problems, write them down. They'll become more manageable. Then work on them one at a time.

26. Don't envy other people. Be happy for what you're working to become.

27. Finding someone who makes you happy is nearly impossible. Decide to be happy and people will be drawn to you.

28. Decide you want to improve, set goals, work to achieve them. You'll notice the good things happening all around you.

29. Enjoy the steps of learning about yourself and then you'll be in a place to help others achieve their goals.

30. Your goals to change your life will be hard work, but you're worth the effort.

If you are not who
You want to be yet, join
the rest of us. Set goals, write
them down, this will help clarify
your path. Perseverance leads to achieving
your goals. Keep working at it. Develop a positive
attitude, an important trait to help you live a happy life.

Achieving Real and Lasting Happiness
(Yes, it is possible!)

31. Happiness will come as you plan and work toward your goals with real desire. You gotta want it.

32. Enjoyment and happiness are not a destination, but a journey of discovery. Choose them over other emotions.

33. One of the best ways to achieve happiness is by hanging out with good, positive people, or seeking uplifting experiences. Happiness and joy are contagious – pass them on.

34. If you are not at peace or contented, choose to find a happy place to go in your head.

35. Allowing others to serve you will make them happy – and you too.

36. Seek for experiences and opportunities that will add joy to your life.

37. You'll have times when you can't fix the struggles in your life. Don't be discouraged or ashamed – be proactive. If you need help, get help from others or from professionals.

38. Bad things happen to everyone. How you handle adversity makes all the difference.

39. Happiness is the state of mind. Love yourself.

40. Wake up every morning and be proud of yourself. Then work to do even better tomorrow.

Money or
possessions don't equal real
happiness. Choosing to be happy
helps you to feel good about your
life. Happiness can be the emotion within
your heart that helps you smile. Some days you
have to grit your teeth, smile, and fake it till you make it.

Financial Security

41. You'll need to identify your needs vs your wants. Fulfilling your needs helps you feel secure. Your wants can overwhelm you and ruin you financially.

42. Banks are not your friend. They are in business to make money. Beware of the hidden charges and fees unless you want to be the means by which they make money.

43. Credit cards can be bad. They can mortgage your future income. Avoid debt like the plague.

44. Buy only what you need starting out. Be patient. Young people expect to have what it took others years to acquire.

45. Buy the best you can afford. Buy cheap and you won't be satisfied because it won't last long.

46. People become wealthy because they don't buy junk that has no value.

47. There are no rewards for having the most toys.

48. You'll never have enough of the stuff you don't need.

49. Purchase what you need with cash. Save up for what you want … and pay for it in cash.

50. A rich man's budget works 100% of the time: If you earn $1.00 – give $.10 away, save $.10, live on $.80. The dime you give away will come back to you in unexpected blessings.

Credit Cards
– a necessary evil?
Mistakes – don't worry,
just keep moving forward.
Financial security – you won't get
There immediately. If a problem can
be fixed with money, it is not really a
problem. If you buy a hamburger for $5.00
on a credit card and don't pay it off at the month's
end, you could eventually pay $25.00 in accumulated
interest for that pricey burger.

Your Value and Worth

good ... value you p... self-worth. n... sense of o... opinion y... ated

51. You are precious. Believe that. You are here to learn, experience, grow, and become the best you can become.

52. Good quality never loses value. You have value. Take the steps to reach the potential that is within you.

53. Hardships are a part of life. The experience you gain is invaluable. Experience the bitter to enjoy the sweet.

54. You are unique. So, enjoy the blessings of who you are and what you can become.

55. Don't let your problems determine who you are, let them help you by learning from them while living out your life.

56. Opinions from others are just observations from their experiences and perspective, not necessarily the truth. Don't allow other people to take away your value and self-worth.

57. Rich or poor is not the sum total of your value. Remembering who you are and what type of person you have the potential to become is also important.

58. The most important gift you have is your self-worth. You will have challenges, pain, and sorrow in your life. If you compare yourself to others you will always come up short and be disappointed. Remember, everyone has challenges.

59. Believe that you count because our maker does not make mistakes, you are not a mistake.

60. Because you have value, because you matter, you will benefit and assist others with the problems in their lives.

Steps To A Happier Life

You can be the
Lamb or the wolf.
You choose one of these
by whichever you feed. The
world will never give you what you want
to be happy. Your self-esteem and self-worth
count, and you can make life a nice place to live.

The Value of Education

61. Education comes from what you learn each day. Use that information to aid you throughout your whole life. Don't waste the opportunity to gain understanding and wisdom.
62. Not everyone attends a university to get an education. Decide what type of education will meet your needs and fits who you are. Everyone needs to get an education of some kind. The choice is yours.
63. It is not the expense of your education, but the importance of what you learn that matters.
64. Schooling is where you start the process of learning. Education is when you value and apply what you have learned.
65. If you believe in yourself, you'll find the type of learning that works for you and your life choices. Be proactive.
66. The lack of education will be the most expensive lesson you will ever learn.
67. A formal education helps. However, is not the sign of success or failure, but of chance. You may need to create your own opportunities for training, if you want them.
68. Pursue the education that gives you value in earning a living.
69. People who are fortunate enough to acquire a great education don't always have good lives. Use your education to do something of value you will enjoy.
70. If you are happy with who you are, life's learning experiences mixed with a good, appropriate education will help you enjoy a beneficial and happy life.

Don't quit
learning After you
leave school. Education
is not what helps you become
wealthy. Knowledge gives you a
head start to earn a good living. Many folk
graduate from the University of Hard Knocks
(or life on the streets) and succeed. Some people
take years to get their college degrees.
Don't be discouraged or quit!

The Expense of Living

71. Make a budget of what you need to live comfortably; then stick to it!
72. Too much stuff clutters your mind, house, and life; don't let belongings make you poor. Let life make you rich.
73. If you can't afford it and buy it anyway, you'll be unhappy with what you have.
74. If you really want some expensive item, wait awhile. Save for it. You might find the desire to possess it will lessen if you take a step back and wait.
75. Once you buy something you don't need, it won't make you happy for long.
76. Garage stuffers are things you won't get rid of, but no longer fit in your house. When you can no longer park two cars in a two-car garage, you have too much stuff.
77. It is less expensive to enjoy what you have and spend your time with who you love.
78. Nothing you possess will ever impress those who have more than you. Don't envy those you think have it all. You'll always be dissatisfied.
79. Real living is not measured by who has the most stuff. Be grateful and content with what you have. If you want extravagant things, plan and save for them. Then you'll appreciate them more.
80. A high-priced life results from having it all and still not being happy.

Things never
made anyone happy.
90% of what people own is
of no real value. People spend the
majority of their lives acquiring too
much stuff. Possessions are bad when they make
you want more than what you have to live comfortably.

Quality of Life, Morals, and Values in Life

81. Good morals never go out of style.

82. To cultivate a good moral character, don't compare yourself to others and don't worry if people don't like you.

83. High moral standards of integrity will make your pursuit of happiness worth the effort.

84. Experience and education give you a quality of life that cannot be taken away.

85. Find value in the daily things that happen to you along life's journey. Do your best regardless of circumstances.

86. Recognize your value and self-worth as a human being. It will help you get through the tough parts of life.

87. Helping others will build your self-esteem and you'll add value to their lives, which in turn will help you enjoy your own.

88. No matter what type of family you came from, you can develop good morals and set a good example for them. Be the inspiration other people need to make tough changes.

89. Your values help you understand the difference between what's important and what's of no worth.

90. What qualities you value – strength, integrity, wisdom, courage, joy – become the principles on which you'll base your behavior. Choose wisely!

What you
value helps you
stand out. Values and
integrity raise your standard of
living. Your unique worth comes from
a lifetime of learning what's important in
life. Self-worth, good morals, and abiding values
will bring you happiness and help you enjoy life to the fullest.

Achieving Success in Life

91. Being successful is 90% failure and 10% success. Don't count the failures.

92. Do something positive each day and for the entire length of your life.

93. You can become successful by cultivating a positive attitude toward what you do, how you do it, or by making a change to something better.

94. Money is not the only reward you receive to feel successful.

95. Successful people pursue worthy goals and cultivate good habits they work on every day.

96. Learn from the past, make a plan, find good mentors, create a routine you can stick to, and then work to obtain your dreams. You can do it!

97. To win at life, you will need slow and steady progress. Success is the reward for consistent hard work toward improvement.

98. You can be happy if you enjoy your own achievements, then work to do even better.

99. Don't measure your success by what others think of you. They will always move the yardstick.

100. You will be successful every day by waking up and doing the very best you can in spite of what life throws your way.

Success

is believing in

yourself, bettering yourself

and those around you. Become

the very best person you can be and

choose to be happy. Don't envy others' lives.

They might look perfect, but it is not always true.

Yes you can

Think positive

Trust in yourself

Never stop learning

Ask for help if you need it

All things are possible

Love to you all,

John

ABOUT THE AUTHOR
John Richard Marsh O'Brien

John Richard Marsh (O'Brien) has earned a Ph.D. from the School of Hard Knocks which makes him more than qualified in the field of overcoming life's hardships and cruelties to finding success, joy, and happiness in life.

John's parents divorced when he was eight and a half years old. His mother, suffering undiagnosed mental issues, kidnapped him and took John to Mexico where she changed his name to Roque (Rōkee) John O'Brien. As a result, John wouldn't answer when his schoolteachers called him Roque. His mom then moved John to Texas, where she met and married a man with three children. John's stepdad was an alcoholic and an abuser. He only had an eighth-grade education and saw no need for John to continue his learning.

The family lived in abandoned houses, with no water, electricity, and slept on mattresses on the floor. His stepdad forced him to sell their personal stuff on the side of the road in order to eat. John began smoking at age thirteen and drinking beer at fourteen, and by tenth grade was asked to leave school. He was told on many occasions he wouldn't amount to much.

John worked menial jobs from age fourteen. At seventeen, he married his pregnant stepsister. Divorced at twenty-two with custody of their children, he moved to Santa Monica and lived as a single parent for eight years. Custody of his three children filled John with a determination to make a better life for them. He began his quest to improve himself and get a good education. It took him fifteen years to earn his Associate Degree. Ultimately, John moved from menial jobs to become a mortgage broker.

Now retired in Southern California, an author and inspirational speaker, John shares 100 simple steps you can take to survive and thrive. He learned to rise above miserable circumstances and find happiness. You can, too.

With gratitude to my readers,

Thank you for reading my little book. I am so pleased you took a chance and read the short pages and the challenges contained within. I hope something from my *Steps To A Happier Life* will touch your heart.

If you would like to comment about the book, please visit my website: jrm-productions.com, and leave your thoughts, issues, or celebrations. Please sign up for my newsletter or follow my blog of life-changing and humorous posts. Any of my friends can comment on my blog, and you are my friends.

I'm always eager to hear if something I said makes a difference in someone else's life. Please feel free to contact me at jrmproductionsco@gmail.com.

www.ingramcontent.com/pod-product-compliance
Lightning Source LLC
Chambersburg PA
CBHW070120110526
44587CB00016BA/2740